THE TRUTH ABOUT BRAIN CHIPS

How Technology Could Determine the Future of Human Intelligence, Society, and the Ethical Dilemmas Ahead

Alejandro S. Diego

1

Table of Contents

Introduction

Imagine a world where the boundary between mind and machine is blurred, where thoughts can be translated into digital signals, and where the essence of being human is no longer confined to flesh and bone. This isn't a distant fantasy or the plot of a science fiction novel; it's the reality we are on the brink of entering. The advent of brain chips is poised to redefine what it means to be human, offering possibilities that were once inconceivable, from restoring lost senses to enhancing cognitive abilities far beyond the natural limits.

In the past few decades, we've witnessed a technological revolution that has transformed our lives in unimaginable ways. Smartphones, artificial intelligence, and the Internet of Things have become integral parts of our daily existence, reshaping how we interact with the world. Yet, as groundbreaking as these innovations are, they pale in comparison to what lies ahead. The next frontier isn't just about smarter devices or faster connections—it's about integrating technology directly into our brains, merging human consciousness with the digital world in ways that challenge our very understanding of self.

Brain-computer interfaces (BCIs) are at the forefront of this revolution, promising to bridge the gap between human thought and machine precision. These tiny, sophisticated devices hold the potential to unlock new dimensions of human capability, enabling us to communicate without words, see without eyes, and even control our emotions with the flick of a neural switch. The implications are profound, not just for individuals but for society as a whole. As we stand on the cusp of this technological leap, it's crucial to understand both the extraordinary benefits and the potential perils that come with it.

The significance of brain chips goes beyond mere technological progress; they represent a fundamental shift in the trajectory of human evolution. For the first time in history, we have the tools to augment our natural abilities, to transcend the limitations of biology, and to explore realms of consciousness that were previously inaccessible. But with this power comes responsibility. As we venture into this new era, we must grapple with complex ethical dilemmas, from the rights of those who choose to remain unenhanced to the potential for unprecedented invasions of privacy.

This book is your guide through the uncharted territory of brain chips, a journey that will take you from the cutting-edge labs where these devices are being developed to the philosophical debates that will shape their future. You'll discover the astonishing possibilities that brain chips offer—restoring sight to the blind, enabling the paralyzed to walk, and even enhancing our cognitive abilities to superhuman levels. But you'll also confront the darker side of this technology, where questions of control, identity, and the very nature of humanity come into play.

As you turn the pages, prepare to have your perceptions challenged and your imagination ignited. The world of brain chips is as thrilling as it is terrifying, filled with promise and peril in equal measure. Whether you're a tech enthusiast, a curious skeptic, or simply someone who wonders what the future holds, this book will take you on a journey into the heart of one of the most exciting—and unsettling—developments of our time. The future of human intelligence is about to be rewritten, and you're holding the key to understanding how.

Chapter 1: The Science Behind Brain Chips

The human brain is often described as the most complex and mysterious organ in the body, a marvel of biology that has fascinated scientists and philosophers for centuries. Yet, at its core, the brain operates much like a highly sophisticated electronic device. It is a vast network of neurons, each one capable of generating tiny electrical impulses that allow us to think, feel, move, and experience the world around us. These electrical signals are the language of the brain, the means by which our thoughts are translated into actions, and our sensations are interpreted into meaning.

Every thought you have, every decision you make, and every movement you initiate begins as an electrical impulse generated by neurons in your brain. These impulses travel through a complex web of neural pathways, sending messages from one part of the brain to another, and ultimately to the rest of your body. It's a system of communication that is both astonishingly fast and incredibly precise, allowing you to react to stimuli in milliseconds and coordinate even the most intricate of actions.

To understand how the brain functions as an electronic device, consider the analogy of a computer. Just as a computer processes information using circuits and transistors, the brain processes information using neurons and synapses. Neurons are the brain's building blocks, each one capable of generating electrical impulses known as action potentials. These action potentials are the brain's version of binary code, the ones and zeros that form the basis of all thought and action.

When a neuron is activated, it sends an electrical impulse down its length, which then jumps across a tiny gap known as a synapse to the next neuron. This process repeats itself countless times throughout the brain, creating a complex web of electrical activity that underpins everything we do. Whether you're reading a book, playing a musical instrument, or simply breathing, your brain is constantly firing electrical signals to make it all happen.

This system of electrical communication is not just limited to the brain. These signals extend throughout the entire body, forming the nervous system—a vast network of nerves that connects the brain to every organ, muscle, and tissue. When you decide to pick up a cup of coffee, for instance, your brain sends an electrical signal down your spinal cord and into the nerves that control your hand. This signal instructs your muscles to contract, allowing you to grasp the cup and bring it to your lips.

But the brain's electrical activity is not just about movement. It also governs your emotions, your memories, and even your personality. When you feel happy, it's because your brain has triggered the release of certain chemicals, which are then interpreted by neurons as feelings of pleasure. When you recall a childhood memory, your brain is reactivating the same neural pathways that were formed when the memory was first created, allowing you to relive the experience in vivid detail.

In essence, the brain is a living, breathing computer, capable of processing vast amounts of information at lightning speed. It's a machine like no other, one that can not only think and reason but also feel and dream. And just like any other electronic device, its function can be influenced—and potentially enhanced—by external inputs. This is the fundamental concept behind brain chips: by tapping into the brain's natural electrical signals, it is possible to restore lost functions, enhance existing capabilities, and perhaps even unlock new levels of human potential.

Brain chips represent a remarkable convergence of biology and technology, designed to interact directly with the brain's natural electrical activity. To understand how these devices work, it's essential to delve into the role of electrodes and the intricate process of translating brain signals into digital information.

At the heart of any brain chip is a network of tiny electrodes, each one meticulously designed to connect with specific neurons in the brain. These electrodes serve as the interface between the organic world of the brain and the digital realm of technology. Their primary function is twofold: recording the electrical signals generated by neurons and sending electrical impulses back into the brain.

When neurons in the brain communicate, they do so by generating electrical impulses known as action potentials. These impulses travel along the neuron's axon, eventually reaching a synapse, where they can trigger the release of neurotransmitters or directly stimulate another neuron. This electrical activity is what allows the brain to process information, make decisions, and control the body.

Brain chips harness this natural electrical activity by embedding electrodes into specific regions of the brain. These electrodes are incredibly small, often thinner than a human hair, allowing them to integrate seamlessly with the brain's delicate neural tissue. Once implanted, these electrodes can record the electrical signals produced by nearby neurons with remarkable precision.

The recorded signals are then transmitted to a chip, usually implanted in the skull or connected wirelessly. This chip acts as a processor, translating the complex patterns of neural activity into digital information. In essence, the chip decodes the brain's electrical language, converting it into a form that computers and other devices can understand.

For example, in the case of a brain chip designed to restore vision to someone who is blind, the electrodes would be implanted in the brain's visual cortex—the area responsible for processing visual information. A camera mounted on the individual's head would capture images, which are then sent to a smartphone or other processing device. This device converts the visual data into electrical impulses that mimic the natural patterns of activity in the visual cortex. The brain chip then sends these impulses directly to the brain, bypassing the damaged eyes or optic nerves, and allowing the person to "see" the world through the camera's lens.

This process of translating brain signals into digital information is not limited to vision. The same principles can be applied to any sensory or motor function controlled by the brain. Whether it's helping a paralyzed person regain control of their limbs or enabling someone to control a computer with their thoughts, the underlying mechanism remains the same: electrodes record the brain's electrical activity, the chip processes and interprets this data, and then sends the appropriate signals back to the brain or an external device.

The implications of this technology are profound. By establishing a direct link between the brain and digital devices, brain chips have the potential to restore lost functions, enhance human capabilities, and even create entirely new ways of interacting with the world. Yet, as with any powerful technology, the possibilities are as vast as they are complex, raising important questions about the future of human-machine integration and the ethical challenges that lie ahead.

The Neuralink N1 chip represents a groundbreaking step in the journey toward integrating technology directly with the human brain. Founded by Elon Musk, Neuralink aims to push the boundaries of what's possible in the realm of brain-computer interfaces (BCIs). The N1 chip, a device the size of a coin, is at the forefront of this effort, designed to interface seamlessly with the brain's natural processes and offer profound new possibilities for restoring and enhancing human capabilities.

Neuralink's vision is ambitious: to create a device that not only repairs broken neural connections but also enhances cognitive function, potentially giving humans new abilities. The N1 chip is the first significant step in realizing this vision. It's designed to be implanted directly into the skull, where it connects to the brain via an array of ultra-thin electrodes—each one thinner than a human hair. These electrodes are meticulously inserted into specific areas of the brain to monitor and influence neural activity.

The implantation procedure itself is as innovative as the chip. Given the delicate nature of the human brain, Neuralink has developed a specialized robot, known as the R1, to handle the intricacies of the operation. This robot is capable of inserting over a thousand electrodes into the brain with unprecedented precision, taking into account the constant movement and pulsation of the living organ. The entire process is automated and designed to be completed in under an hour, minimizing the risks associated with traditional brain surgery.

Once implanted, the N1 chip begins its work. It records the electrical signals generated by neurons, sending this data wirelessly to a computer or smartphone for processing. The chip is also capable of sending electrical impulses back into the brain, influencing neural activity in targeted ways. This bidirectional communication is what allows the chip to restore lost functions, such as sight or movement, by bypassing damaged areas of the brain and creating new pathways for information to flow.

One of the most remarkable features of the N1 chip is that it is entirely invisible once implanted. The chip replaces a small portion of the skull, sitting flush with the surface of the head, making it undetectable from the outside. It is powered wirelessly, charging through the skin without the need for any external ports or connectors. This design ensures that the chip can function continuously without interrupting the user's daily life.

The N1 chip's initial applications are focused on treating neurological conditions, such as paralysis, blindness, and other brain-related disorders. However, the long-term vision for Neuralink is far more expansive. Musk and his team envision a future where the N1 chip can be used to enhance cognitive abilities, improve memory, and even enable direct brain-to-brain communication. These advancements could redefine what it means to be human, blurring the line between natural and artificial intelligence.

The Neuralink N1 chip is more than just a piece of technology; it is a glimpse into the future of human evolution. As we continue to explore the possibilities of brain-computer interfaces, the N1 chip stands as a pioneering achievement, opening doors to a new era where the mind and machine are inextricably linked. The implications of this technology are vast and varied, promising to change the way we think, feel, and interact with the world around us.

Chapter 2: The Potential Benefits

The potential for brain chips to restore lost functions is one of the most compelling aspects of this emerging technology. By directly interfacing with the brain's neural networks, brain chips offer the possibility of restoring vision, movement, and other sensory functions that have been lost due to injury or disease. This technology, which once seemed like the stuff of science fiction, is rapidly becoming a reality, with early experiments in animals paving the way for human applications.

Consider the case of vision restoration. For individuals who have lost their sight due to damage to the eyes or optic nerves, the brain's visual cortex remains intact but underutilized. A brain chip, such as the Neuralink N1, can be implanted in the visual cortex, allowing the brain to bypass the damaged structures and receive visual information directly from a camera or other external sensor. This information is then processed and converted into electrical impulses that the brain can interpret as visual images. Early experiments with this technology have shown that it is possible to simulate basic vision, giving hope to those who have been blind from birth or who have lost their sight later in life.

Movement restoration is another area where brain chips hold immense promise. For individuals who have been paralyzed due to spinal cord injuries, the connection between the brain and the muscles is severed, rendering the body immobile. However, the brain's motor cortex, which controls movement, remains functional. By implanting electrodes in this region, a brain chip can capture the brain's intent to move and transmit this information to an external device that can then stimulate the muscles, bypassing the damaged spinal cord. In animal experiments, researchers have successfully restored movement in paralyzed limbs by using brain chips to reconnect the brain's motor signals with the body's muscles.

One notable example is the work Neuralink has done with pigs. In these experiments, electrodes were implanted in the pigs' brains to record and stimulate neural activity. By capturing the brain's signals, researchers were able to predict and influence the movement of the pigs' limbs, demonstrating the potential for brain chips to restore mobility in paralyzed patients. These early successes in animals have laid the groundwork for future human trials, where similar techniques could be used to help people who have lost the ability to walk or use their arms.

Beyond vision and movement, brain chips also have the potential to restore other sensory functions, such as hearing or touch. For example, a brain chip could be used to restore hearing by bypassing damaged auditory nerves and sending sound information directly to the brain's auditory cortex. Similarly, for individuals who have lost their sense of touch due to nerve damage, a brain chip could be used to simulate tactile sensations by stimulating the appropriate areas of the brain.

The implications of these advancements are profound. For the first time, individuals who have been told that their conditions are irreversible may have a chance to regain lost functions. The ability to see, move, hear, or feel again would not only improve their quality of life but also offer them a level of independence that was previously unimaginable. As this technology continues to develop, it holds the promise of transforming the lives of millions of people around the world.

However, the journey from animal experiments to widespread human application is still in its early stages. While the results so far are encouraging, much work remains to be done to ensure that these technologies are safe, effective, and accessible to those who need them. But with each new breakthrough, the dream of restoring lost functions through brain chips moves closer to becoming a reality, offering hope to those who have lost so much and opening up new possibilities for what it means to be human.

As brain chips continue to advance, their potential reaches far beyond the restoration of lost functions. These devices hold the promise of enhancing normal human abilities, opening up new frontiers in vision, mood control, memory, and more. The concept of brain enhancement is both exhilarating and thought-provoking, presenting possibilities that could fundamentally alter the human experience in ways that are only beginning to be explored.

Imagine a world where your vision is no longer limited by the natural capacity of your eyes. With the integration of a brain chip, you could gain extraordinary visual abilities—seeing with a clarity that surpasses even the sharpest human eyesight. You might have the power to zoom in on distant objects, similar to adjusting the lens of a camera, or perceive colors and details beyond the typical human spectrum. Some might even be able to see in complete darkness by tapping into infrared or other non-visible wavelengths. Such enhancements could revolutionize industries like medicine, engineering, and the arts, giving professionals unprecedented tools to excel in their fields.

Beyond physical enhancements, brain chips could offer a new level of control over our emotions and mood. Currently, treatments for conditions like depression or anxiety involve medications that adjust brain chemistry. A brain chip, however, could provide an instant, customizable way to manage emotions. Imagine being able to dial down stress during a hectic day or boost your mood during a challenging moment—all with a simple mental command. This technology could lead to a society where emotional well-being is managed as easily as physical health. Yet, it also raises deep ethical questions about the authenticity of our feelings and the potential consequences of such power.

Memory enhancement is another area where brain chips could revolutionize human capabilities. Memory, as it naturally exists, is imperfect—subject to fading, distortion, and loss over time. A brain chip could change that by acting as an external storage device for the mind. Imagine being able to recall every detail of a conversation, a book you read years ago, or even a fleeting moment of inspiration with perfect accuracy. Beyond just recalling memories, brain chips could also allow us to augment them, creating vivid, multi-sensory experiences from past events or even crafting entirely new ones.

However, the implications of such enhancements extend beyond the individual to society as a whole. If some people have access to enhanced cognitive abilities while others do not, we could see a new kind of inequality emerge—one based not on wealth or education, but on access to brain technology. Those with enhanced brains might excel in ways that outpace their unenhanced peers, creating a divide that could reshape social, economic, and even political structures.

The concept of brain enhancement also forces us to reconsider what it means to be human. If our thoughts, memories, and emotions can be manipulated or enhanced by technology, where do we draw the line between our natural selves and the augmented versions we could become? This raises profound philosophical and ethical questions about identity, free will, and the nature of human experience.

As we move closer to a future where brain enhancement becomes a reality, it is crucial to consider not only the incredible possibilities but also the potential risks and ethical dilemmas. The power to enhance human capabilities could lead to unprecedented advances in knowledge, creativity, and well-being. Yet, it also comes with the responsibility to navigate these changes thoughtfully, ensuring that the technology is used in ways that benefit all of humanity, rather than creating new forms of division or exploitation.

In exploring the possibilities of brain enhancement, we stand at the threshold of a new era—one where the limits of the human mind are no longer defined by biology alone. The choices we make in this era will shape the future of our species, determining whether we harness this technology to uplift all of humanity or allow it to deepen existing inequalities. The journey into this new frontier is just beginning, and it promises to be as exciting as it is challenging.

Chapter 3: Ethical and Practical Concerns

The development of brain chips, like many advanced medical and technological innovations, relies heavily on extensive research and testing, much of which involves the use of animals. This necessity, however, has sparked significant controversy due to the ethical implications of conducting invasive experiments on living beings.

Animal testing is a deeply entrenched practice in scientific research, often viewed as essential for ensuring the safety and effectiveness of new technologies before they are applied to humans. In the context of brain chips, animals are used to test the viability of these devices in a living brain, to observe how neural tissue reacts to implanted electrodes, and to study the effects of these chips on behavior and brain function. However, the use of animals—particularly in such complex and potentially painful procedures—raises ethical questions that are difficult to ignore.

Critics argue that the suffering inflicted on animals during these experiments is unjustifiable, especially when alternatives, such as computer modeling or cell cultures, might be available. Brain chip research often involves implanting electrodes into the brains of animals, which can lead to significant discomfort, stress, and even death. For example, companies like Neuralink have been criticized for the number of animals that have died as a result of their experiments. Leaked reports have suggested that some of these deaths may have been due to rushed procedures, driven by the pressure to achieve quick results. Such incidents highlight the potential for ethical lapses when the drive for innovation outpaces the commitment to humane treatment of test subjects.

The ethical implications of using animals in brain chip research extend beyond the immediate harm to individual animals. They touch on broader questions about the moral status of animals and the responsibilities of researchers to minimize harm wherever possible. The central ethical dilemma is whether the potential benefits to humans—such as restoring lost sensory functions or enhancing cognitive abilities—justify the suffering inflicted on animals. Proponents argue that these benefits, which could eventually improve the lives of millions of people, outweigh the costs. However, opponents counter that inflicting suffering on sentient beings for the sake of technological progress is inherently wrong, particularly when the long-term outcomes for humans are still uncertain.

Moreover, there are concerns about the transparency and oversight of such experiments. Ethical standards for animal research vary widely across countries and institutions, and there is often a lack of clear, enforceable guidelines specifically tailored to emerging technologies like brain chips. This lack of regulation can lead to situations where the welfare of animals is compromised in the pursuit of scientific and commercial goals. To address these issues, there is a growing call for more rigorous ethical standards and greater transparency in the reporting of animal research, particularly for technologies that have the potential to profoundly impact human life.

As brain chips become more sophisticated and integrated into human cognition, they present new and significant security risks. The prospect of hacking a brain chip, while once the domain of science fiction, is now a very real concern that carries potentially devastating consequences.

A brain chip, by its very nature, acts as an interface between the human brain and digital technology. This connection, while offering incredible opportunities for enhancement and restoration of functions, also makes the brain vulnerable to external threats. If a hacker were to gain access to a brain chip, the potential for harm is immense. They could, in theory, manipulate the thoughts, memories, and perceptions of the person using the chip, fundamentally altering their sense of self and autonomy. For instance, a hacker could implant false memories, change a person's emotional state, or even control physical movements by sending rogue signals through the chip.

The implications of such an attack are profound. Beyond the immediate harm to the individual, there are broader concerns about the potential for large-scale manipulation. Imagine a scenario where a hacker could influence the decisions of a group of people or even an entire population by altering their thoughts and perceptions. This could be used for political gain, to incite violence, or to create widespread panic. The possibility of such scenarios underscores the need for robust security measures to protect the integrity of brain chips and the privacy of their users.

In addition to the threat of hacking, there is also the risk of more subtle forms of manipulation. Brain chips, by design, interact with the neural circuitry that governs our thoughts, feelings, and behaviors. This raises the possibility that the technology could be used to influence individuals in ways that are not immediately apparent, but nonetheless significant. For example, companies could design chips that subtly influence consumer behavior, such as by altering preferences or creating desires for certain products. Governments or other entities might use brain chips to monitor and control populations, suppress dissent, or enforce conformity.

These risks highlight the need for strict ethical guidelines and regulatory frameworks to ensure that brain chips are used in ways that respect individual autonomy and privacy. It also underscores the importance of developing secure, transparent, and accountable systems for managing the data generated by these devices, to prevent their misuse for nefarious purposes.

The commercialization of brain chips introduces another layer of ethical complexity, particularly regarding the potential for corporate control and the socio-economic divide that could emerge as a result of unequal access to these technologies.

As brain chips transition from experimental devices to marketable products, there is a significant risk that companies could exploit this technology for profit in ways that are not in the best interest of consumers. For instance, companies might implement subscription-based models, where users are required to pay ongoing fees to access or maintain certain features of their brain chips. This could extend to essential functions, such as memory recall or mood regulation, effectively turning aspects of human cognition into commodities that can be bought and sold. The idea that individuals might need to pay to retain access to their own thoughts, memories, or emotions raises profound ethical concerns about autonomy and the commodification of the human mind.

Additionally, there is the potential for companies to deliberately limit the capabilities of older chips, encouraging users to upgrade to newer, more expensive versions. This practice, often seen in the tech industry with smartphones and other devices, could lead to situations where people feel pressured to continually invest in new technology just to maintain their cognitive abilities. Such practices could exploit vulnerable individuals, particularly those who may already be dependent on brain chips for essential functions, creating a cycle of financial burden that is difficult to escape.

The introduction of brain chips also risks exacerbating existing social and economic inequalities. If access to brain chips is determined by wealth or social status, those who can afford the technology will have significant advantages over those who cannot. Enhanced cognitive abilities could lead to better job opportunities, higher incomes, and greater social mobility for those with brain chips, while those without access could find themselves increasingly marginalized and disadvantaged.

This divide could deepen over time, as the gap between the enhanced and unenhanced widens, leading to a society where brain enhancement becomes a prerequisite for success. Such a scenario raises important questions about fairness and equity, and whether society should take steps to ensure that brain enhancement technologies are accessible to all, regardless of economic status.

In addressing these challenges, it is essential to consider the broader societal implications of brain chip technology. Policymakers, ethicists, and the public must engage in discussions about how to balance the potential benefits of brain chips with the need to protect individual rights and promote social justice. As brain chips become more prevalent, it will be crucial to ensure that their use is guided by principles of fairness, equity, and respect for human dignity, to prevent the emergence of a new form of technological elitism.

These ethical and security concerns highlight the complex landscape that surrounds the development and deployment of brain chip technology. While the potential benefits are vast, so too are the risks, and it will take careful consideration and regulation to navigate these challenges in a way that maximizes the positive impact of brain chips while minimizing their potential for harm.

Chapter 4: The Future of Brain Chips

The future of brain chips presents a vision where the boundaries between human cognition and artificial intelligence become increasingly blurred. As these chips evolve, the possibility of integrating them with AI could lead to an unprecedented transformation in human capabilities and society at large. This integration isn't merely about enhancing human abilities; it suggests a profound shift in what it means to be human, potentially pushing our evolution in a new and uncharted direction.

Elon Musk, through his company Neuralink, has been one of the most vocal proponents of this future. He has warned of the dangers posed by rapidly advancing AI, suggesting that without a way to merge with technology, humans risk being left behind. Musk's vision is not just to keep pace with AI but to create a future where humans and AI are inextricably linked. The brain chip, in this scenario, becomes a critical tool that allows human intelligence to expand beyond its natural limits, enabling us to interact with AI as if it were an extension of our own minds.

The implications of such a merger are staggering. If human cognition could be enhanced and integrated with AI, the possibilities would be endless. We might access information instantly, perform complex calculations in seconds, and even enhance our creativity by collaborating with AI in real-time. Learning could become instantaneous, as knowledge could be uploaded directly to our brains. The ability to process and understand vast amounts of data could revolutionize fields such as science, medicine, and the arts, leading to breakthroughs that are currently unimaginable.

However, the integration of AI with the human brain also raises significant ethical and philosophical questions. If AI becomes a part of our cognitive processes, it blurs the line between human and machine, leading to fundamental questions about identity and agency. At what point do our thoughts remain ours, and when do they become influenced or even controlled by the AI integrated into our brains? This raises concerns about the potential loss of free will and the authenticity of human experience.

As brain chips and AI become more integrated into society, the social and economic impacts could be profound. The widespread adoption of brain-enhancing technology might create new forms of inequality. Those who can afford such enhancements would likely gain significant advantages in various aspects of life, from education to employment, leaving those without access at a severe disadvantage. This could create a society where a new form of inequality emerges—one based not on wealth alone but on access to cognitive enhancement.

In such a world, the divide between the enhanced and the unenhanced could deepen, leading to a new class of second-class citizens. Those without brain chips might find themselves marginalized, unable to compete with their enhanced counterparts in an increasingly demanding world. This could exacerbate existing social and economic inequalities, leading to a society where success and social mobility are increasingly determined by access to technology rather than talent or effort.

The commercialization of brain chips adds another layer of complexity. Companies that develop and control these technologies might exploit them for profit, creating a market where only the wealthy can afford the most advanced enhancements. This could lead to a situation where the benefits of brain chips are concentrated among a small, privileged group, further entrenching social divides and creating new forms of exclusion.

Beyond the immediate social and economic implications, brain chips also open up possibilities that challenge our understanding of life and death. One of the most speculative yet intriguing ideas is the concept of digital resurrection—the notion that a person's consciousness could be backed up and potentially restored after death. Brain chips could record and store the data of our brains, capturing the neural patterns that define our thoughts, memories, and personality. In theory, this data could be used to recreate a person's consciousness in a digital format, allowing them to "live" on after their physical body has ceased to function.

The idea of digital resurrection, however, raises profound philosophical and ethical questions. If a digital copy of a person's consciousness is created, is that copy truly the same person, or is it merely a sophisticated replica? What does it mean for the nature of identity if one's consciousness can be preserved and restored in a new form? And if immortality can be achieved in a digital realm, how does that change our understanding of life and death?

Moreover, the pursuit of digital immortality could further exacerbate social inequalities. If only the wealthy can afford to back up their brains and achieve digital resurrection, immortality could become a luxury available only to a privileged few, deepening the divide between the rich and the poor. This raises ethical concerns about the fairness of such a technology and its potential to create new forms of inequality.

As brain chips continue to evolve, these possibilities—both real and speculative—will increasingly shape the discourse around human evolution, social structures, and the future of our species. The integration of human minds with AI, the potential for social and economic disparities, and the pursuit of digital immortality all represent the cutting edge of this technological frontier. As we move forward, the choices we make will determine how these technologies are integrated into our lives and what kind of future we build with them.

Chapter 5: The Dark Side of Brain Chips

As brain chips become more advanced and integrated into our lives, privacy concerns emerge as one of the most pressing issues. The potential for these devices to be used for invasive advertising and the unprecedented access they could provide to our most intimate thoughts raises significant ethical and moral questions. When brain chips have the ability to interface directly with our minds, the boundary between personal privacy and corporate interest becomes dangerously thin.

Imagine a world where your thoughts are no longer entirely your own. Brain chips, by their very design, could have the capability to monitor and record neural activity. This data, which could include everything from your emotions to your deepest desires, might be harvested and analyzed by companies looking to tailor their products and services to your subconscious needs. Advertising, already pervasive in the digital age, could take on a new form—one that is not just targeted based on your browsing history or purchase patterns but directly influenced by your brain's activity. The moment you experience a craving, a brand could present an offer, making it nearly impossible to distinguish between your genuine desires and those subtly implanted by external forces.

This raises profound ethical concerns about autonomy and free will. If companies have direct access to your thoughts, the potential for manipulation becomes real and immediate. Your preferences, decisions, and even your sense of self could be shaped by algorithms designed to influence your behavior for profit. This level of intrusion into the human mind goes far beyond the current issues of data privacy and targeted advertising, touching on the very essence of personal freedom and identity. The ethical implications are vast, questioning whether it is right for any entity—be it a corporation or government—to have such deep access to an individual's inner world.

Moreover, the loss of privacy is not just a theoretical concern but a potential reality that could redefine how we perceive and interact with the world around us. The trust between individuals and the technology they use could be eroded, leading to a society where people are constantly aware that their thoughts are being monitored and possibly manipulated. This could create a pervasive sense of paranoia and mistrust, fundamentally altering the way we live our lives.

As we explore the possibilities of brain chips, we must also consider the broader implications of becoming increasingly reliant on machines. There is a significant risk that as we integrate more technology into our bodies, we may begin to lose our sense of agency and humanity. Brain chips offer the promise of enhanced abilities and improved lives, but they also pose the danger of making us overly dependent on technology to the point where it dictates our behavior and decisions.

If brain chips become ubiquitous, there is a potential for them to influence not just individual behavior but societal norms and expectations. For instance, in a world where cognitive enhancement becomes the standard, those who choose not to or cannot afford to enhance themselves may be viewed as inferior or less capable. The pressure to conform to a technologically enhanced norm could lead to a loss of individuality, where people feel compelled to adopt brain chips to remain competitive or socially acceptable. This societal pressure could erode the diversity of human experience, reducing the rich tapestry of individual differences to a homogenized norm dictated by technology.

Furthermore, the reliance on brain chips could lead to a deeper existential crisis—a loss of what it means to be human. As we delegate more of our cognitive functions to machines, we may begin to question our own value and purpose. If a brain chip can enhance creativity, problem-solving, and emotional regulation, what is left of the uniquely human experience? The risk is that in our quest to improve and optimize every aspect of our lives, we may inadvertently strip away the very qualities that make us human—our capacity for empathy, our ability to make mistakes, and our need for connection and meaning.

The potential consequences of a society where brain chips dictate behavior are profound. Such a society might prioritize efficiency and productivity over creativity and emotional depth, valuing the enhanced capabilities of brain chips over the messy, unpredictable nature of human thought and emotion. This could lead to a world where human relationships and interactions are increasingly mediated by technology, with people becoming more isolated and disconnected from one another.

In the end, the promise of brain chips must be balanced against the potential risks to privacy, autonomy, and humanity. As we move forward into this new frontier, it is crucial to engage in thoughtful discussions about how to protect the core values that define our humanity. The choices we make today will determine whether brain chips enhance our lives or lead us down a path where we lose touch with what it truly means to be human.

Chapter 6: Navigating the Ethical Dilemmas

As brain chip technology advances and becomes more integrated into society, the role of regulation becomes increasingly critical. Government and regulatory bodies must step in to ensure that these powerful technologies are developed and used in ways that protect individual rights, promote public safety, and uphold ethical standards. The stakes are high, as the potential for both immense benefits and significant risks is enormous.

The importance of government oversight in the development and deployment of brain chips cannot be overstated. These devices interact directly with the human brain, influencing thoughts, emotions, and behaviors. Without proper regulation, there is a danger that brain chips could be misused, leading to violations of privacy, autonomy, and even fundamental human rights. Governments must work closely with scientists, ethicists, and industry leaders to establish clear guidelines and standards for the development, testing, and deployment of brain chips.

One of the key areas where regulation is needed is in the testing and approval process for brain chips. Given the profound impact these devices can have on human cognition, it is essential that they undergo rigorous testing to ensure their safety and efficacy. Regulatory bodies must establish protocols for clinical trials that address not only the technical aspects of the devices but also their psychological and ethical implications. This includes evaluating the long-term effects of brain chip implantation and ensuring that participants in trials fully understand the risks involved.

In addition to safety standards, there must be clear guidelines regarding the ethical use of brain chips. This includes regulations to protect individuals from coercion or exploitation, particularly in vulnerable populations. For example, policies should be in place to prevent employers from requiring brain chip enhancements as a condition of employment or to protect individuals from being pressured into using brain chips to remain competitive in their field. There should also be safeguards to ensure that brain chips are used in ways that respect individual autonomy and that their use is always voluntary and fully informed.

Another critical area for regulation is data privacy. Brain chips have the potential to collect vast amounts of data about an individual's thoughts, emotions, and behaviors. This data is incredibly sensitive and must be protected from unauthorized access or misuse. Governments must establish strict data protection laws that ensure individuals have control over their data and that companies are held accountable for how they collect, store, and use this information. This includes the right for individuals to access their data, request its deletion, and be informed about how it is being used.

The ethical challenges posed by brain chips extend beyond the realm of regulation and into the broader question of how society should balance technological progress with ethical considerations. As brain chip technology advances, there is a temptation to push the boundaries of what is possible without fully considering the ethical implications. However, it is crucial that progress is guided by a strong ethical framework that prioritizes human dignity, autonomy, and the common good.

One of the key challenges in balancing progress with ethics is determining the acceptable limits of brain enhancement. While the potential benefits of brain chips are immense, there is a risk that the technology could be used in ways that undermine fundamental human values. For example, the pursuit of cognitive enhancement could lead to a society where people feel pressured to constantly upgrade their brains to keep up with others, leading to a loss of individuality and a devaluation of those who choose to remain unenhanced. Society must engage in a collective dialogue to determine where the line should be drawn between beneficial enhancements and those that pose a risk to our humanity.

The role of society in shaping the ethical use of brain chips cannot be understated. While governments and regulatory bodies have a critical role to play, it is ultimately up to society as a whole to decide how these technologies should be used. This requires an informed and engaged public that understands the implications of brain chip technology and is willing to participate in the debate about its future. Public education and discourse are essential to ensuring that the development of brain chips is guided by the values and priorities of the broader society, rather than being driven solely by technological capability or commercial interests.

In conclusion, the regulation of brain chip technology is essential to ensuring that its development and use are safe, ethical, and aligned with the values of society. Governments must establish clear guidelines and standards for the testing, approval, and deployment of brain chips, while also protecting individual rights and privacy. At the same time, society must engage in a broader conversation about the acceptable limits of brain enhancement and the ethical implications of this powerful technology. By working together, we can harness the potential of brain chips in ways that enhance human life while respecting our fundamental values and preserving our humanity.

Chapter 7: The Path Forward

As brain chip technology continues to advance, public awareness and education become increasingly crucial. The implications of integrating such powerful devices into the human brain are vast, touching on everything from personal identity to societal structures. Ensuring that the public is well-informed about these developments is essential for fostering informed discussions and making collective decisions about how this technology should shape our future.

The introduction of brain chips into society presents a complex web of ethical, psychological, and social challenges. These devices have the potential to alter fundamental aspects of human life, yet many people may not fully understand what brain chips are, how they work, or what their widespread adoption could mean. To bridge this gap, there is a pressing need for comprehensive public education that demystifies brain chip technology and explains both its benefits and risks.

Public education efforts should aim to provide clear, accessible information about the science behind brain chips, how they are developed, and their potential applications. This includes explaining the basics of how brain chips interface with neural activity, the kinds of enhancements or restorations they can offer, and the ethical dilemmas they pose. By making this information widely available, people can better grasp the significance of brain chip technology and its potential to reshape various aspects of life, from healthcare to personal privacy.

Moreover, education should go beyond the technical aspects to include discussions about the broader societal implications. People need to understand not only how brain chips work but also how their adoption could impact social norms, economic opportunities, and personal autonomy.

For instance, if brain chips become a common tool for enhancing cognitive abilities, what does that mean for those who choose not to use them, or for those who cannot afford them? How might such technology affect our concepts of free will, individuality, and equality? Addressing these questions in public forums, schools, and through media can help foster a more informed and engaged society.

Encouraging informed discussions about the future of brain technology is equally important. As brain chips move from experimental stages to widespread use, it's vital that people from all walks of life participate in the conversation about how this technology should be used and regulated. This involves creating spaces—whether physical or digital—where individuals can share their thoughts, concerns, and hopes about brain chips in a constructive and respectful manner.

These discussions should be inclusive, drawing on perspectives from various disciplines, including science, ethics, law, and philosophy, as well as from the general public. By engaging in dialogue, society can collectively determine the acceptable boundaries of brain chip technology, deciding where to draw the line between enhancement and intrusion, between innovation and exploitation. It's through these conversations that we can ensure that the development of brain chips aligns with societal values and priorities, rather than being driven solely by technological or commercial imperatives.

Looking further ahead, the implications of brain chips raise profound questions about the future of human intelligence and what it means to be human. As these devices become more sophisticated, they have the potential to redefine human cognition, enabling capabilities that far surpass our natural limits. This could usher in a new era of human evolution, where intelligence is no longer constrained by biology but can be enhanced and expanded through technology.

In this future, brain chips might enable us to access vast amounts of information instantly, communicate telepathically, or experience augmented realities that blend seamlessly with the physical world. The line between human and machine could blur, leading to a hybrid form of intelligence that combines the best of both. This could lead to extraordinary advancements in knowledge, creativity, and understanding, potentially solving some of the world's most pressing problems.

However, the same technology that offers such promise also carries the risk of leading us into a dystopian future. If brain chips are used to control or manipulate people, or if they exacerbate existing inequalities, the result could be a society where freedom, privacy, and individuality are eroded. The potential for misuse by governments, corporations, or other powerful entities is significant, especially if the technology is not carefully regulated and ethically guided.

The speculative nature of this future adds to the urgency of public awareness and education. People need to be equipped with the knowledge and critical thinking skills necessary to navigate the complexities of brain chip technology. They must be prepared to engage with the ethical and philosophical questions that this technology raises, from the nature of consciousness to the limits of human enhancement.

In conclusion, the future of brain chips will be shaped not just by the scientists and engineers who develop them, but by the society that embraces or rejects them. Public awareness and education are essential in ensuring that this technology is understood, debated, and ultimately governed in a way that reflects the values and aspirations of humanity. The potential for brain chips to redefine human intelligence is immense, offering both the promise of a new era of human evolution and the risk of a dystopian future. How we respond to these challenges will determine the path we take, and whether we use this powerful technology to enhance our lives or risk losing what makes us truly human.

Conclusion

As we stand on the brink of a technological revolution with the advent of brain chips, the future we envision is one of unprecedented possibilities and equally profound challenges. Throughout this exploration, we have delved into the science behind brain chips, the ethical dilemmas they present, and the potential they hold to reshape our very understanding of what it means to be human.

We began by examining the incredible promise of brain chips to restore lost functions and enhance human capabilities. From offering sight to the blind to enabling paralyzed individuals to move again, these devices have the potential to transform lives in ways that were once the realm of science fiction. We also explored the exciting, yet unsettling, idea of enhancing normal human functions—granting us superhuman abilities such as enhanced memory,

63

mood control, and even direct integration with artificial intelligence. These advancements could usher in a new era of human evolution, where the limits of biology are transcended by technology.

However, with such great power comes significant responsibility. The ethical implications of brain chip technology are vast, touching on issues of privacy, autonomy, and the very essence of human identity. The potential for invasive advertising, the risk of hacking, and the possibility of creating a society divided by access to brain enhancements all raise serious concerns about how this technology will be used and who will benefit from it. We also confronted the speculative but deeply philosophical concept of digital resurrection, pondering the questions of immortality and what it truly means to be "alive."

The role of regulation emerged as a critical factor in guiding the development and deployment of brain chips. Governments and regulatory bodies must establish clear guidelines to ensure that brain chips are used safely and ethically, protecting individuals from exploitation and safeguarding their most intimate thoughts and experiences. At the same time, society as a whole must engage in ongoing discussions about the acceptable limits of brain enhancement and the potential consequences of merging human minds with machines.

Public awareness and education are essential in this journey. As brain chips move from the laboratory to everyday life, it is crucial that people are informed and engaged in the conversation about how this technology will shape our future. Informed discussions will allow us to collectively determine the boundaries of this new frontier, ensuring that progress is balanced with respect for human dignity and values.

In reflecting on the future, we find ourselves at a crossroads. The choices we make today will determine whether brain chips become tools that enhance our humanity or lead us down a path where we lose touch with what makes us truly human. The delicate balance between embracing new technologies and preserving our core values is one that requires careful consideration and thoughtful action.

As we look forward, we must ask ourselves not just what we can do with this technology, but what we should do. The potential for brain chips to change the world is immense, but so too is the responsibility to use this power wisely. By approaching this new era with both excitement and caution, with both innovation and ethics, we can ensure that the future of brain chips is one that benefits all of humanity—enhancing our lives while preserving the very essence of who we are.

www.ingramcontent.com/pod-product-compliance
Lightning Source LLC
LaVergne TN
LVHW051614050326
832903LV00033B/4495